GERALD W. PARKER

Get Excited or Stay Broke Forever

First published by ISBN Services 2025

First edition

ISBN: 979-8-90030-801-2

This book was professionally typeset on Reedsy.
Find out more at reedsy.com

Contents

Acknowledgments

This book is dedicated to everyone who has ever felt overlooked, underestimated, or pressed for time. May it ignite your inner fire and serve as a powerful reminder that it's never too late to achieve power, focus, and a vibrant life.

I extend my deepest gratitude to the exceptional men whose mentorship profoundly impacted my life and inspired these very words: Fernando Ramirez, Zik Steward, Brian House, Steven Johnson, Randy Christensen,Steve Schulz, Andre Vaughn, Andamo Tolson, Bishop Charles Dingle, Bill Andreoli, Bishop Ernest Sutton, Mike Randolph, Rubin Young, Edward Simmons, Emilio Jean-Louis, Pastor David Schmall, and Brian Beane. Thank you.

Stay excited. Stay dangerous.

— Dr. Gerald W. Parker

1

Chapter 1: Discipline = Freedom

We've been lied to. For too long, we've been sold a story that discipline is a prison. A rigid, joyless cage where fun goes to die. We see the person who wakes up early, hits the gym, and sticks to their budget as a robot, a boring sacrifice to a life they aren't truly enjoying. We chase fleeting moments of "freedom" in a life of ease, comfort, and convenience, and we wonder why we end up feeling stuck, unmotivated, and broke.

That's the illusion.

Real freedom is not the absence of structure; it's the mastery of it.

Think about it. Is the undisciplined person free? The one who has no control over their money, their time, or their health? They are a slave to every impulse, every distraction, and every fear. They are not free to pursue their dreams because they are too busy putting out fires and reacting to the chaos of a life lived by chance. They are a prisoner in their own life, shackled by their own lack of ownership.

Now, consider the disciplined person. They have the freedom to say "no" to a night of pointless scrolling because they are committed to building something. They have the freedom to walk away from a draining conversation because they know their energy is valuable. They have the freedom to take a risk in their career because they have built a financial fortress.

Their freedom wasn't granted; it was earned. It's the direct result of a thousand small, conscious decisions. Every time you chose to do the hard thing instead of the easy one, you didn't just build a habit—you broke a chain.

Discipline is the engine of your liberation. It's the ability to act in your own best interest, even when you don't feel like it. It's choosing your long-term vision over your short-term impulse. This isn't about punishment; it's about purpose.

The world wants you to be a victim of your circumstances. They want you to believe that success is a lottery ticket, a lucky break, or a miracle you're waiting for. But radical ownership is your way out. The miracle isn't coming for you. The miracle is you. Your discipline is the proof.

You are not waiting on a miracle. The miracle is you. Own it.

From this day forward, stop seeing discipline as a tax on your joy. See it as the ultimate act of self-love. It's a commitment to your future self that you will no longer tolerate mediocrity. It's the decision to build, to lead, and to dominate.

The question isn't whether you have the discipline to be free. The question is, can you afford to stay a prisoner?

You cannot build a life that pays you back without a routine that supports it. In the next chapter, we will build the foundation for that routine and begin to stack your wins, one small act of ownership at a time.

2

Chapter 2: Build a Strong Routine

You read the last chapter. You got excited. You agreed that discipline is the path to freedom, not the opposite. Now what? You can't just stand there staring at your mountain of goals. You need a map. That map is your routine.

Most people see a routine as a leash. A boring, repetitive act that kills creativity and spontaneity. They want to "wing it" every day, and they get to the end of the day exhausted, having accomplished nothing of substance. They are a victim of decision fatigue—every small choice, from what to eat for breakfast to what to work on first, drains their mental energy. They live in a state of reaction, not action.

A strong routine is not a leash; it's a launchpad.

It is the strategic framework that automates the small decisions so you can save your energy for the big ones. A solid routine is your daily declaration that you are in control. It's the blueprint for building a life that pays you back, not just in money, but in purpose and power. Think about the most successful people you know. They don't "wing it." They have a system. They own their mornings. They know exactly what they are doing and why they are doing it. They have turned discipline from a conscious effort into an unconscious habit.

Your routine is your greatest weapon against chaos. It's a series of small, intentional victories that build an unstoppable momentum. It's the daily work that makes you undeniable.

The Four Pillars of a Bulletproof Routine

Your routine doesn't have to be perfect, but it must be purposeful. Here are the four pillars you must master:

1. **Own Your Morning: The Ultimate Power Play** This is the most crucial part of your day. The person who wins the morning almost always wins the day. This isn't just about waking up early; it's about what you do in that first hour. It's about getting up without hitting snooze, moving your body, and planning your top three priorities before the world has a chance to invade your focus. You are not just waking up—you are taking possession of your day. This sacred time, before emails and texts start flying, is your window to get ahead. You can use it to read, to meditate, to visualize your success, or to simply enjoy the quiet. The point is, you are a leader, and a leader starts their day on their terms, not on someone else's.
2. **Strategic Work Blocks: The Engine of Progress** You can't just be busy; you have to be productive. A strong routine includes dedicated blocks of "deep work" where you focus on one mission or project with zero distractions for 60-90 minutes. This is where real progress is made. This is where you get ahead of the competition. This is where you build. A lot of people fall into the trap of multitasking, but all they are doing is a half-effort on multiple fronts. High-performance is about focus. It's about building a fortress

of concentration so you can complete a task you've been avoiding and get a powerful win.

3. **Fuel Your Mind and Body: The Non-Negotiable Foundation** You cannot operate at a high level if you are running on empty. A solid routine includes intentional time for feeding your mind (e.g., reading 5-10 pages of a self-growth book) and fueling your body (e.g., tracking what you eat and moving your body). Your health and your wealth are not separate. They are intrinsically linked. You must treat your body and your mind like the high-performance machines they are. When you show up for your body, you are showing up for your goals.
4. **The End of Day Audit: The Loop of Improvement** Your routine isn't complete until you review your performance. Before you shut down your screens (at least 30 minutes before bed), take a few minutes to reflect. What did you do well? Where did you slip? What is the game plan for tomorrow? This is how you learn from your mistakes and start the next day with a plan, not a prayer. You are not just living; you are building a system for success.

Don't over complicate this. Start small. The "Short Daily Discipline Checklist" we've included in this book is your starting point. It's a simple, powerful tool to help you get your first wins. Check off what you complete each day and watch your confidence grow. Small wins lead to big transformations.

You are no longer allowed to just "hope" things get better. You are going to build it. It's time to move from being a victim of your habits to becoming the architect of your destiny.

In the next chapter, we'll tackle one of the biggest roadblocks to building a routine: fear. We'll show you why the most courageous act isn't the absence of fear, but the decision to **"Do It Scared."**

3

Chapter 3: Do It Scared

You've got the vision. You've got the plan. You've even started to build a routine. Now you're standing at the edge of the diving board, looking down. Your heart is pounding. Your palms are sweating. And that little voice in your head, the one you've listened to your whole life, is screaming: "Don't jump! You're not ready! What if you fail?"

That's fear. It's the gatekeeper to your greatness. And if you're waiting for it to go away before you take action, you will stay stuck, scared, or silent forever.

Let's be clear: fear has a purpose. It's the ancient alarm system that kept our ancestors from becoming lunch for a saber-toothed tiger. That kind of fear keeps you safe. But the fear we're talking about—the fear of judgment, of failure, of not being 'ready'—isn't protecting you from a predator. It's caging your potential.

We've been fed another lie: that courage is the absence of fear. That the most successful people in the world are fearless. That's a fantasy. Courage isn't the absence of fear; it's action *in the presence of fear*. It's knowing you are terrified but doing it anyway.

I'll never forget the feeling of my hands shaking before I hit 'publish' on my very first article. Fear wasn't just a passenger in my car; it had a death grip on the steering wheel. A voice screamed, "Who are you to say this? Everyone will think it's terrible!" But I knew the regret of not trying would be worse. I closed my eyes, took a breath, and clicked the button. It wasn't perfect, and it didn't change the world overnight, but in that moment, it changed me. I had chosen action over fear.

Fear is a passenger in your car, not the driver. It can sit in the backseat and scream all it wants, but you are the one with your hands on the wheel. You decide the destination. You decide when to hit the gas. The moment you hand over the keys to fear is the moment you become a prisoner to your own potential.

Don't confuse procrastination with preparation. Don't mistake perfectionism for progress. These are just masks that fear wears to keep you comfortable and small. Procrastination is fear's favorite tactic. It whispers, "Just wait until you have more information." Perfectionism says, "This isn't good enough yet. Wait until it's perfect." The world doesn't need a perfect plan. It needs you to have persistent fire.

So, how do you break the grip of fear when it feels like a canyon to cross? You don't jump across. You build a bridge, one brick at a time, using your 'Do It Scared' Toolkit.

Your 'Do It Scared' Toolkit

- **The 2-Minute Rule:** Don't commit to a full task. Commit to just two minutes of the feared activity. Don't commit to writing the first chapter; commit to opening the document and writing for just two minutes. Don't commit to running a 5k; commit to putting on your shoes and walking out the door for two minutes. Momentum is the antidote to fear, and it begins with the smallest possible action.

- **Fear-Setting:** Grab a piece of paper or open a document and ask yourself three questions: What is the absolute worst-case scenario if I do this? How could I recover if that happens? What is the cost of inaction if I do nothing at all? This exercise often reveals that the vague fear in your head is far more terrifying than the actual worst-case scenario.
- **Identify the First Physical Action:** Instead of "take the first step," get more granular. What is the very first physical movement required? To have that difficult conversation, the first step is picking up your phone. To start a business, it might be typing a domain name into a registrar. This makes the overwhelming feel manageable.

The cost of inaction is always greater than the pain of a mistake. The regret of not trying will haunt you far more than the memory of a stumble. A mistake can be corrected, but a missed opportunity can never be recovered.

Your future self is waiting for you to get a move on. They are waiting for you to stop playing small, to stop wishing, and to stop waiting for the perfect moment.

It's time to light that fire within you, push past fear, and take radical ownership of your future. You're no longer allowed to stay stuck, scared, or silent. The choice is yours.

4

Chapter 4: Money Mindset

Let's talk about money. The word alone makes people uncomfortable. We've been taught to believe that money is the root of all evil, that talking about it is rude, and that being "broke" is a condition you're born into—not a choice. That's another lie. The truth is, money is just a tool. It's a scoreboard. It's a reflection of your mindset and your decisions, and if your scoreboard is empty, it's not because the game is rigged. It's because your strategy is broken.

Your financial reality is not a matter of circumstance; it's a matter of mindset. A "broke" mentality is a belief system that you're a victim of your financial situation. It's an attitude of scarcity, a constant feeling of "not enough." A "wealth" mentality is a belief system that you are in control of your financial destiny. It's an attitude of abundance, a powerful understanding that you are the source of your own success.

You are a magnet. Your beliefs are either attracting or repelling wealth. Most people have a rusted-out, weak magnet. They say they want to be rich, but their thoughts and actions scream scarcity. They complain about the cost of everything.

They justify their lack of discipline by saying, "I just can't afford it." They view money as a finite resource that is always slipping away. A wealthy mindset sees money as a tool to create, to invest, to build, and to impact. It views resources as abundant, and it trusts that hard work and smart decisions will generate more of them.

The Poverty Traps of a Broke Mindset

To build a new mindset, you have to tear down the old one. Here are the core beliefs of a broke mentality that are keeping you stuck:

1. **The "One Day" Fallacy:** A broke mindset lives in a fantasy future where money will just appear. "One day, I'll get a raise." "One day, I'll win the lottery." "One day, I'll start that business." This is a passive, reactive mindset. It refuses to take radical ownership and instead outsources its financial future to luck, chance, or someone else's generosity. The wealthy mindset knows there is no "one day." There is only today. They don't wait for a miracle; they create one through consistent, intentional action.
2. **The "Entitlement" Trap:** This is the belief that you are owed something. You feel like you deserve a high-paying job, a perfect life, or a certain level of success without putting in the work. You blame others for your lack of progress—the economy, your boss, your family. This is the opposite of radical ownership. A wealth mindset knows that nothing is owed to them. Success is earned, not given. It is the result of relentless discipline, sacrifice, and a commitment to perpetual self-improvement.

3. **The "Scarcity" Mindset:** This is a zero-sum game mentality. You believe that for someone else to win, you have to lose. You are secretly resentful of other people's success. You think that money is a limited pie and if someone else takes a big slice, there's less for you. This kind of thinking repels abundance. A wealth mindset knows that the pie is unlimited. There is more than enough for everyone. The success of others is not a threat; it's proof of what's possible.

The Blueprint for a Wealth Mindset

Building a wealth mindset is an act of defiance. It's a deliberate choice to rewire your brain and believe in your ability to generate resources. Here is the blueprint:

1. **Stop Blaming, Start Building:** You must take 100% radical ownership of your financial situation, right here, right now. It doesn't matter what your circumstances are. It doesn't matter what you've been through. The only thing that matters is what you do from this day forward. Stop making excuses and start making money. Stop complaining and start creating.
2. **Redefine Your Relationship with Money:** Stop seeing money as a source of fear and anxiety. Start seeing it as a tool for freedom. Money gives you the freedom to choose, the freedom to create, and the freedom to give back. The goal isn't just to be rich. The goal is to use your resources to build a life that pays you back in purpose, passion, and power.
3. **Invest in Yourself:** The most profitable investment you

will ever make is in your own skills, knowledge, and growth. Your earning potential is directly tied to your value in the marketplace. You want to get paid more? Become more valuable. Read books, take courses, and learn from mentors. Don't wait for someone else to invest in you; you are your own best asset.

4. **Practice Gratitude:** A powerful way to shift from a scarcity mindset to an abundance mindset is through gratitude. Every day, acknowledge the money you have, no matter how small. Be grateful for your income, your health, your home, and the opportunities around you. Gratitude rewires your brain to focus on what you have, not what you lack. It opens the door to more.

Your mindset is the thermostat of your financial future. If it's set to "broke," you'll stay broke. If it's set to "wealth," you will begin to attract and create resources. This isn't magic; it's a manual for action.

It's time to burn the broke beliefs. In the next chapter, we'll do just that, with a direct and no-nonsense breakdown of the exact beliefs you need to replace to build a life that is both profitable and purposeful.

By integrating your suggestions, I will now build Chapter 5 to be more illustrative, psychologically grounded, and actionable. I will incorporate real-world scenarios, a deeper look into the origins of "broke beliefs," and provide clear, immediate action steps for the reader.

5

Chapter 5: Broke Beliefs vs. Wealth Beliefs

In the last chapter, we established that money is a mindset. Now, it's time to get surgical. We're going to expose the parasitic beliefs that have been eating away at your potential and replace them with a powerful blueprint for wealth. This isn't an academic exercise; it's a war for your financial freedom. On one side, you have the broke beliefs—the excuses, the rationalizations, and the mental traps. On the other, you have the wealth beliefs—the actions, the ownership, and the momentum. The choice is yours.

First, let's be clear about something. These broke beliefs aren't character flaws; they are often inherited scripts. We learn them from our parents, absorb them from our social circles, or adopt them as defense mechanisms after a financial setback. While they may not be your fault, it is your responsibility to challenge and rewrite them. The first step is recognizing them for what they are: outdated software that needs an upgrade.

Broke Belief #1: "I can't afford it." This is the phrase of a victim. It's a statement of powerlessness that hands your financial future over to your current circumstances. It shuts down all possibilities and accepts scarcity as your final destination. It tells the world, "I have no control."

Wealth Belief #1: "How can I afford it?" This is the phrase of a leader. It's a statement of radical ownership that opens up a world of creative solutions. It shifts your brain from a passive state of "no" to an active state of "how." This belief doesn't mean you should buy everything you want; it means you are actively seeking ways to create the resources to get what you need and what you desire. It is the language of an entrepreneur, a problem-solver, and a builder.

The Story of Two Friends: Imagine two friends, both with a passion for building websites, see a powerful online course that would transform their skills and their careers. The course costs $1,500. The first friend immediately says, "I can't afford it." The conversation ends. The second friend, after a moment of thought, pulls out a notebook and starts brainstorming: "Okay, how could I make this happen? I could sell my old camera on eBay, pick up two extra freelance shifts, or maybe they have a payment plan." The first friend stayed broke. The second found a way.

Broke Belief #2: "The rich are greedy/lucky." This is the language of resentment. This belief serves one purpose: to justify your lack of success by demonizing others who have achieved it. It's a zero-sum mentality that says if someone else is winning, you must be losing. This kind of thinking repels the very abundance you claim to want.

Wealth Belief #2: "The rich are problem-solvers who create value." This is the language of opportunity. You understand that wealth is a result of solving problems for a large number of people. You see successful people not as a threat but as a roadmap. Their wealth is proof of what's possible. Instead of resenting them, you study them. You ask, "What problems are they solving? How can I create value?"

Broke Belief #3: "I'll save what's left over." This is the "hope" strategy. It assumes that money will magically be left over at the end of the month after you've spent on everything else. The reality is, there's always something else to spend on. This belief ensures that your savings account—and your future—will stay empty.

Wealth Belief #3: "I pay myself first." This is the "build" strategy. You treat your savings and investments as a non-negotiable expense. The first percentage of every paycheck goes directly into an account you don't touch. This isn't an option; it's a command. This simple act of discipline builds a foundation of financial security and teaches you to live on what's left, not save what's left.

Do This Now: Stop reading. Open your banking app right now and set up an automatic transfer of just 1% of your next paycheck to your savings account. You won't miss it, but you will have just started the most important wealth-building habit of your life.

Broke Belief #4: "I need to know everything before I start." This is the language of inaction. It's a sophisticated form of procrastination disguised as intelligence. You spend your life in analysis paralysis, waiting for the perfect market, the perfect idea, or the perfect moment. You are not waiting for a miracle; you are waiting for a guarantee, and guarantees don't exist in the real world.

Wealth Belief #4: "I start before I'm ready." This is the language of momentum. You understand that imperfect action beats perfect inaction every single time. You know that the market and the opportunity will change whether you act or not. You are not a spectator; you are a player. You learn by doing, you fail forward, and you correct your course as you go. You build the ship while you're sailing.

Momentum Challenge: Identify one small financial or career goal you've been procrastinating on. In the next five minutes, take the smallest possible step toward it. Send the email. Register the domain name. Write the first sentence of the business plan. Imperfect action creates momentum.

The choice is yours. You can cling to the broke beliefs that are keeping you stuck, or you can begin the daily, disciplined work of adopting the wealth beliefs that will set you free. This is not about being born into money; it's about choosing a mindset that builds it.

The work begins now.

6

Chapter 6: Short Daily Discipline Checklist

Words are just words. Ideas are just ideas. A great philosophy is useless without a plan to execute it. You've read about radical ownership, the power of a strong routine, and the necessity of doing it scared. Now, it's time to build.

Before you even look at this list, let's kill the excuses your brain is already manufacturing.

- **"I don't have time."** False. This entire list can be accomplished in under 60 minutes, total. You have the time; you've just been giving it to less important things.
- **"This is too simple to work."** That's the point. Complexity is the enemy of consistency. These aren't magic tricks; they are foundational acts of discipline that build the bedrock for bigger wins.
- **"My day is too unpredictable."** All the more reason to control what you can. This checklist isn't about controlling your entire day; it's about winning the first hour and the last hour, which gives you the strength to handle the chaos

in between.

Discipline isn't about grand, life-altering acts. It's about showing up for the small habits, every single day. This checklist is your blueprint for momentum. Each checkmark is a small win. And small wins, stacked on top of each other, create a streak. A winning streak.

This isn't just something to read; it's a tool to use. It's your daily challenge to prove to yourself that you are in control. So, stop reading. Take this challenge and get to work.

Short Daily Discipline Checklist

[ ] Wake up without hitting snooze

- *The Win:* You start your day with a victory over your weaker self. You take immediate ownership of your morning.

[ ] Make your bed

- *The Win:* You start your day by accomplishing a task and creating an environment of order. It's your first win before you've even left the room.

[ ] Move your body (even 10 minutes)

- *The Win:* You flood your body with energy and build the habit of physical discipline. This is a direct deposit into your mental and physical health.

[ ] Plan your top 3 priorities

- *The Win:* You eliminate decision fatigue and ensure you focus on what truly matters, not just what's urgent. You are a leader, not a reactor.

[ ] Track what you eat

- *The Win:* You bring awareness to your choices and take control of the fuel you put into your high-performance machine.

[ ] Read 5-10 pages of a self-growth book

- *The Win:* You commit to perpetual growth, ensuring you are always learning and expanding your perspective.

[ ] Complete a task you've been avoiding

- *The Win:* You kill procrastination, build momentum, and reclaim the mental energy that task was consuming. This is a direct deposit into your confidence account.

[ ] Review your wins

- *The Win:* You train your brain to focus on progress, not just problems. You build a foundation of gratitude and acknowledge your growth.

[ ] Shut down screens 30 mins before bed

- *The Win:* You protect your sleep, the foundation of all energy and discipline, and end your day on your own terms.

How to Use This Tool

Don't just read this page. Use it.

- Take a picture of the checklist with your phone right now. Set it as your lock screen for the next 7 days.
- Write it on a sticky note and put it on your bathroom mirror.
- Commit to a 7-day streak. Don't think about doing this forever. Just focus on winning this week. Track your score each day. The goal is to build a winning streak and make discipline a habit.

Scoring Your Day:

- Complete 5+ items = You're moving.
- Complete 7+ items = You're winning.
- Complete all 9 items = You're on fire.

Small wins lead to big transformations. Track the streaks. Stay consistent

7

Chapter 7: Discipline Tracker

You've read the words. You've accepted the challenge. You've embraced the idea that discipline equals freedom, and you've seen the power of the Small Daily Discipline Checklist. Now, it's time to build.

A winning streak doesn't happen by accident. It is built one day at a time, one checkmark at a time, one decision at a time. The problem with relying on your memory or a vague feeling of "I'm doing well" is that it's easy to lie to yourself. It's easy to forget the days you slipped, the mornings you hit the snooze button, and the tasks you avoided.

This tracker is your truth.

It is your accountability partner, your personal scoreboard, and the undeniable evidence of your commitment. It forces you to confront your actions and celebrate your wins. It is the tool that turns your intention into a habit and your habit into an unbreakable system.

Use this page to hold yourself accountable. Pin it on your wall. Stick it on your refrigerator. Put it somewhere you can see it every single day. The goal is simple: to fill every box and build a streak you are proud of. Don't break the chain.

The work begins with a single check mark:

7-Day Discipline Tracker

"Discipline is my daily decision."

Instructions: Use this tracker to hold yourself accountable for the small, daily wins that build unstoppable momentum. At the end of each day, check the boxes you completed and calculate your score. The goal is to build a winning streak.

Day	Wake Up (No Snooze)	Make Bed	Move Body	Plan Top 3	Track Food	Read 5 Pgs	Complete Hard Task	Review Wins	Screens Off	Daily Score
Mon	☐	☐	☐	☐	☐	☐	☐	☐	☐	
Tue	☐	☐	☐	☐	☐	☐	☐	☐	☐	
Wed	☐	☐	☐	☐	☐	☐	☐	☐	☐	
Thu	☐	☐	☐	☐	☐	☐	☐	☐	☐	
Fri	☐	☐	☐	☐	☐	☐	☐	☐	☐	
Sat	☐	☐	☐	☐	☐	☐	☐	☐	☐	
Sun	☐	☐	☐	☐	☐	☐	☐	☐	☐	

Scoring Key:

5-6/9: You're building momentum.

7-8/9: You're winning the day.

9/9: You're in complete control.

End of Week Reflection

This is your time to get real. Be honest with yourself and prepare for your next week of winning.

My Biggest Win This Week Was:

The Habit That Was Easiest to Stick To:

The Habit I Slipped on the Most Was:

Why Did I Slip? What Was the Obstacle?

My #1 Focus for Next Week Will Be:

8

Chapter 8: Weekly Goals and Results Page

You've mastered the daily game. You've embraced discipline as the foundation of your freedom, and you've started to build an unbreakable streak of small, daily wins. But a great day is just a single brick. To build a fortress, you need a blueprint for the week.

This Weekly Goals and Results Page is the strategic bridge between your daily effort and your long-term vision. It transforms your raw energy into directed power. A lot of people live in a state of reaction, simply moving from task to task without a clear purpose. That's a recipe for burnout and stagnation. You are not here to survive; you are here to dominate. And domination requires a plan.

Before you fill this out, understand the difference between a goal and a wish.

A **wish** is vague: 'Make more progress on my side hustle.' A **goal** is a target you can hit: 'Finish and publish the first three modules of my online course.'

Your weekly goals must have a clear finish line. They must

be actions you can definitively check off as 'done.' Don't write down aspirations; write down deliverables. This simple weekly format helps you align your goals and reflect on results. It keeps your vision clear and execution on point. You will not get to the end of the week wondering where your time went. You will have a clear, undeniable record of your progress. It's time to stop hoping and start hunting. The work begins now.

Weekly Goals and Results Page

My #1 Focus for the Week:

My Top 3 Priority Goals for the Week: 1. 2. 3.

My Daily Action Plan to Win the Week: (For each weekly goal, what is the one daily action I must take?)

- Action for Goal 1: ____ __________
- Action for Goal 2: ____ __________
- Action for Goal 3: ____ __________

End of Week Reflection & Scoreboard

- **Goal 1:** Did I achieve it? (Yes/No) *What worked: What didn't:*
- **Goal 2:** Did I achieve it? (Yes/No) *What worked: What didn't:*
- **Goal 3:** Did I achieve it? (Yes/No) *What worked: What didn't:*

My Overall Score: (1–10)

Lessons Learned: What is the most important lesson I learned this week?

Game Plan for Next Week: Based on this week's results, what is my new #1 focus?

Here's What This Looks Like in Action for Someone Starting a Coaching Business:

My #1 Focus for the Week: Launch my website.

My Top 3 Priority Goals for the Week:

1. Finish and publish the "Services" and "About Me" pages.
2. Set up the payment processing system.
3. Write and schedule the 3 social media posts announcing the launch.

My Daily Action Plan:

- Action for Goal 1: Spend 60 minutes writing/editing website copy.
- Action for Goal 2: Complete one step of the payment setup checklist.
- Action for Goal 3: Draft one social media post.

Of course. This is a powerful and essential chapter that provides the "why" behind all the "what" of the previous chapters. It's the perfect place to transition from pure discipline to inspired action.

You've created a great compass. Here is an expanded version

that adds more reading material, deepens the psychological context, and provides even more clarity for the reader, transforming it from a checklist into a comprehensive workshop.

9

Chapter 9: Purpose Discovery Journal & Realignment Checklist

You've been building. You've been disciplined. You've been doing the hard work of building a routine and chasing down your goals. You've proven you can climb. But let me ask you a question that stops most high-achievers in their tracks: **Are you climbing the right mountain?**

Momentum without purpose is just motion. It's the difference between a high-performance race car with a driver who knows the track and a runaway vehicle hurtling toward a cliff. You can have all the discipline, all the courage, and all the money in the world, but if it's not in service of a purpose that truly lights your fire, you will end up at the finish line feeling unfulfilled and empty. This is the great trap of the modern world: achieving a life you never actually wanted.

Most people treat purpose like a lottery ticket—something you hope to find one day, fully formed, under a rock. That's a lie sold to you to keep you passive. **Purpose isn't found; it's built.** It's clarified through consistent, honest self-inquiry and the courage to realign when life inevitably throws you off course. It is an active, ongoing process of excavation.

This Purpose Discovery Journal and Realignment Checklist is your compass and your shovel. It is designed to help you get quiet, get honest, and get clear on your "why." This is not a passive exercise; it's a manual for action. It's the tool that ensures every checkmark you make and every goal you hit is taking you closer to the life you were meant to live.

It's time to stop just moving and start leading—starting with yourself. Let's find your true north.

The Purpose Discovery Journal: A Meeting With Your Future Self

Treat this journaling practice not as a chore, but as the most important meeting of your week. This is your strategic session with the CEO of your life: you. Your task is to get brutally honest about what drives you. Don't write what you think sounds good; write what feels true.

Journaling Prompts:

1. **What Were You Born to Do?** Think back to your childhood, before the world told you who you should be. What did you do for fun that felt effortless? What activities made you lose track of time? Maybe it was organizing your toys (a sign of a systems builder), telling elaborate stories (a sign of a creator), or taking things apart to see how they worked (a sign of an engineer). What did you love so much you'd do it for free? This is a clue to your most natural, authentic state of being.

2. **What Are You Naturally Good At?** This is your unique genius. What skills do people consistently ask you for help with? Is it simplifying complex ideas? Mediating arguments? Fixing things? Organizing chaotic events? Pay attention to the problems people bring to you. Your natural talents are often so second-nature to you that you don't even recognize them as a skill. List them out. This is the raw material of your purpose.
3. **What Makes You Angry?** Your frustration is a compass. What injustices, inefficiencies, or problems in the world make you feel a deep sense of frustration or righteous anger? Is it seeing talented people waste their potential? Is it convoluted corporate bureaucracy? Is it a lack of financial literacy in your community? That anger is a powerful signal. It points directly to a problem you are uniquely equipped, and motivated, to solve. Your purpose often lies on the other side of your greatest frustration.
4. **Who Do You Want to Help?** Purpose is never just about you; it is always in service of others. Who are the people you feel a magnetic pull to serve, lead, or inspire? Is it young entrepreneurs? Struggling artists? Families in your community? Getting specific about *who* you want to help clarifies your *what* and *why*. Your purpose gains power when it is attached to a clear mission for others.
5. **If You Had No Fear of Failure or Judgment, What Would You Do?** Answer this question quickly, without overthinking. If you knew you could not fail, and no one would judge your choice, what would you dedicate your life to? Write down the first thing that comes to mind. This question bypasses the logical, conditioned part of your brain and speaks directly to your soul's ambition. This is often the

purest signal of your true north.

The Purpose Realignment Checklist: Your Tactical Reset Button

Life is a constant process of falling off course and correcting. This checklist is your tool for those moments when you feel stuck, unmotivated, or lost. Use it weekly or whenever you feel the drift.

[ ] **Revisit your "Why."** Go back and read your answers to the journal prompts. Reconnect with the core purpose you identified. The daily grind can make you forget why you started. This act of remembrance is a powerful anchor that pulls you back to what truly matters.

[ ] **Audit your environment.** Your environment is either pushing you toward your purpose or pulling you away from it. Do the people, places, and things around you support your mission or drain your energy? Look at the five people you spend the most time with. Look at the information you consume. Does your environment reflect the person you are trying to become?

[ ] **Cut the distraction.** Purpose requires focus. What is one thing you can eliminate from your life (a habit, a person, a commitment) that is not in service of your purpose? Saying "no" to the wrong things is just as important as saying "yes" to the right ones. Be ruthless in protecting your energy and attention.

[ ] **Take one small, aligned action.** Purpose is built through action, not just thought. Do something today that directly connects to your purpose, no matter how small. Make the call.

Write the first sentence. Send the email. Register the domain. Small, aligned actions build momentum and prove to yourself that you are serious.

[ ] **Speak your purpose aloud.** Tell one person you trust what you are building and why. This act of declaration makes it real. It moves your purpose from a private thought to a public commitment. Speaking it gives it energy and invites accountability, both from yourself and from others.

10

Chapter 10: The Unbreakable Day: A Blueprint for Winning Your Time

You have a compass. You've done the hard, internal work to find your true north. But a compass is useless if you don't use it to navigate the terrain of your daily life. The gap between knowing your purpose and living your purpose is where most people fail. They have a destination but no map.

This chapter is your map. It's a blueprint for structuring your day not around what is urgent, but around what is **important**. It's a system designed to protect your focus, multiply your output, and ensure that your best energy is always directed toward the goals that matter most. We are going to stop letting the day happen *to* us and start telling the day what it is going to be. This is how you build an unbreakable day.

The Four Blocks: A Structure for Domination

An unbreakable day is built on four distinct, purpose-driven blocks of time. Each block has a specific mission. By separating your day into these zones, you eliminate decision fatigue and create a rhythm that builds momentum.

1. The Foundation Block (First 60-90 Minutes of Your Day)
This is your personal boot camp. This block is non-negotiable and happens before you give your energy to anyone else. It's where you win the first battle of the day: the one against your own inertia. This is a direct application of your **Short Daily Discipline Checklist**.

- **Mission:** To build personal momentum and fortify your mindset.
- **Key Actions:** Wake up without snooze, make your bed, move your body, read, and plan your top 3 priorities for the day.
- **The Rule:** No email. No social media. No news. This time is for you and you alone. You are building your foundation, not reacting to the world's chaos.

2. The Deep Work Block (90-120 Minutes of Peak Energy)
This is the most sacred time of your day. It is a pre-scheduled, uninterrupted sprint dedicated exclusively to your **#1 Weekly Goal**. This is where you make meaningful progress on the mountain you've chosen to climb. For most people, this is in the morning when willpower and focus are at their highest.

- **Mission:** To make significant, measurable progress on your most important long-term goal.
- **Key Actions:** Writing the book, building the business,

learning the new skill, coding the app. This is for creation, not administration.

- **The Rule:** Zero distractions. Phone on silent and in another room. Close all unnecessary tabs. Put up a sign on your door if you have to. You must defend this block with your life.

3. The Shallow Work Block (The Rest of Your Workday) This is for the necessary but less demanding tasks of your day. It's for the meetings, the emails, the phone calls, and the administrative work that keeps the lights on. By batching these tasks together, you prevent them from bleeding into and contaminating your deep work time.

- **Mission:** To efficiently manage the administrative and collaborative parts of your work.
- **Key Actions:** Responding to emails, attending meetings, running errands, and completing routine tasks.
- **The Rule:** Be efficient, not perfect. Use this time to clear the decks, but don't let it expand to fill your entire day. It serves your deep work, not the other way around.

4. The Recharge Block (The End of Your Day) This is where you intentionally shut down and refill your tank. True high performance isn't about working all the time; it's about recovering with the same intensity that you work. This block is for family, health, and peace.

- **Mission:** To recover, connect with loved ones, and prepare your mind and body for the next day.
- **Key Actions:** Eating dinner with family, spending quality time with your kids, reading for pleasure, hobbies, and

shutting down all screens 30-60 minutes before bed.

- **The Rule:** When you are done with work, be done. Don't check your email one last time. Don't ruminate on the day's problems. Be present where you are. Your recovery is a critical part of your process.

A Sample Blueprint: The Unbreakable Day in Action

- **Foundation Block (6:00 AM - 7:30 AM):** Wake up, make bed, 30-minute workout, read 15 pages, review weekly goals, and plan the day's top 3 priorities.
- **Deep Work Block (8:30 AM - 10:30 AM):** 120 minutes of uninterrupted writing for a new book project. Phone is off.
- **Shallow Work Block (10:30 AM - 5:00 PM):** Team meetings, responding to emails, client calls, and administrative tasks.
- **Recharge Block (5:00 PM onwards):** Workout, family dinner, playtime with kids, read a novel, screens off by 9:30 PM.

This isn't a rigid prison; it's a flexible framework. Your times may vary, but the principles remain the same. Protect your foundation, prioritize your deep work, manage your shallow work, and commit to your recovery. This is how you stop living a life of reaction and start building a life of intention. This is how you win the day.

11

Chapter 11: Circle Audit Worksheet

We've talked about owning your mornings, your money, and your mind. But there's a powerful force shaping your future that you may not have taken full ownership of yet: your circle.

The people you spend the most time with are the average of what you are, and the ceiling of what you can become. Your circle determines your ceiling. It's a harsh truth, but it's a non-negotiable one. You can have all the discipline and drive in the world, but if you're surrounded by people who are content with mediocrity, who drain your energy, or who constantly doubt your vision, you will eventually be pulled down to their level. You are not a victim of your circumstances, and that includes the people you choose to let into your life.

This isn't just a motivational concept; it's a law of human nature. Scientists call it **"emotional contagion."** You unconsciously absorb the mindsets, beliefs, and standards of the people you are around most often. Their energy, whether it's ambitious and positive or cynical and draining, literally seeps into your subconscious.

Think of your life as a garden. Some people are fertilizer—

they nourish you, help you grow, and celebrate your success. Others are weeds—they compete for your resources, drain your energy, and choke out your potential. A great gardener isn't mean; they are strategic. They intentionally cultivate what they want to grow and ruthlessly remove what they don't. This audit is you tending to your garden.

The Radical Mindset of the Circle Audit

This Circle Audit Worksheet is not about being a bad friend; it's about being a great leader of your own life. This is not a passive exercise in judgment; it is a strategic act of radical ownership. To do this correctly, you must approach it without emotion. This is a business audit, not a loyalty test. You are simply evaluating your team for performance and potential. Who is stretching you, and who is draining you?

The goal is simple: to upgrade your circle, and in doing so, upgrade your life. It's time to stop surviving and start building a life that pays you back.

Circle Audit Worksheet

"Your circle determines your ceiling. Upgrade your circle. Upgrade your life."

Instructions: Write down the names of the 5-10 people you spend the most time with. For each person, be brutally honest in your assessment.

Name

How Do They Stretch Me? (Growth, Inspiration, Accountability)

How Do They Drain Me? (Negativity, Gossip, Doubt, Complaining)

My Action Plan (Amplify, Limit, or Evolve)

1.

2.

3.

4.

5.

The 3 Tiers of Action: Amplify, Limit, and Evolve

Once you've identified the impact of each person, your action plan falls into one of three categories:

- **Amplify:** For the people who stretch you. This is simple: be intentional about investing more time and energy here. Schedule a call. Set up a coffee meeting. Send them a text thanking them for their influence. Double down on what's working.
- **Limit:** For people who consistently drain you. This doesn't require a dramatic confrontation. It's about creating distance. Become less available. Shorten the length of your phone calls. Stop saying "yes" to every invitation. You are reclaiming your time and energy by strategically creating space.
- **Evolve:** For relationships that are a mix, or for people you care about but who have draining habits. This is where a

direct, honest conversation is needed. This isn't an attack; it's you setting a new boundary. Use a simple script like: "I'm really focused on a new set of goals right now, and I'm trying to be more positive and disciplined with my time. I've noticed our conversations often turn to [Gossip/Complain ing]. I value our friendship, but I need to keep my energy focused. Can we try to talk more about [Goals/Ideas/Positive Topics]?"

Reflection & Final Action Plan

This is where you turn raw data into a strategic plan. Get quiet and get honest.

- **My Biggest Insight from This Audit Is:**
- **The People I Will Amplify This Week Are:**
- **The People I Will Limit This Week Are:**
- **The Action I Will Take to Evolve a Key Relationship Is:**
- **My #1 Commitment to My Circle This Week Is:**

12

Chapter 12: Burn the Boats Action Plan

In 1519, the Spanish conquistador Hernán Cortés landed on the shores of Veracruz, Mexico, with his army. A few hundred men, thousands of miles from home, stood on the beach staring into a dense, alien jungle. They could hear strange birds, smell the woodsmoke of a civilization they couldn't comprehend. And behind them, the familiar creak of the ships—their only link to the world they knew, their only way back.

Then, the order. It wasn't a suggestion. It was a command that defied all logic. "Burn the boats." Imagine the shock, then the dawning horror, and finally, the terrifying clarity. As the flames licked the hulls and the masts cracked and fell, every man on that beach understood: the option to go back was gone. Their past was turning to ash. The only way home was through the empire in front of them.

Your life is the conquest. For too long, you have been living with a fleet of ships parked behind you—your escape routes, your excuses, your safety nets. Every time a challenge gets tough, you retreat to a comfortable past. Every time a new habit feels hard, you run back to the old, easy one. You've been living a life where success is an option, not a necessity.

It's time to burn the boats.

The Psychology of No Escape

This wasn't just a dramatic gesture; it was a masterclass in human psychology. Cortés was creating what psychologists now call a **"commitment device."** By eliminating the option of retreat, he short-circuited his men's ability to waste energy on doubt, hesitation, or second-guessing.

When you have a Plan B, you will subconsciously give Plan A less than 100% of your effort. Your mind will always keep one foot in the safety of the boat. Burning the boats forces your brain to stop calculating escape routes and start dedicating all of its resources to solving the problem in front of you. It's the ultimate tool for manufacturing focus.

This is the ultimate act of radical ownership. This is where you move from saying you're committed to proving it. You must eliminate the option of returning to the person you were. You must leave no room for doubt or retreat. This is not a time for half-measures. It is a time for total, unapologetic commitment.

The Boats to Burn

- **The Boat of Excuses:** This is the boat of "I'm too tired after work," "I don't have the startup capital," or "I'm not a natural at this." These aren't reasons; they are well-rehearsed stories you tell yourself to justify inaction. Burn the alibis that have kept you small.

- **The Boat of "Someday":** Burn the illusion that you have unlimited time. "Someday" is a lie. It's a fantasy where your goals are achieved without action. There is only today, and it is the only day you have to build your future.
- **The Boat of Complacency:** Burn the comfort zone that has been a prison disguised as a palace. Your growth happens in discomfort, not in convenience. A comfortable life is a dying one.
- **The Boat of Unproductive Habits:** This is the boat of the 9 PM Netflix binge that kills your morning energy. It's the boat of the 30-minute social media scroll that turns into two hours. These habits aren't just wasting your time; they are actively rowing you back to the shore of your old life.
- **The Boat of Limiting Relationships:** This is the boat of the friend who meets your new business idea with a sigh and a list of all the ways it could fail. It's the family member who constantly reminds you to "be realistic." They aren't bad people; they are just anchors chained to your ambition.
- **The Boat of Low Standards:** Burn the belief that mediocrity is acceptable. You must raise your standards to an unshakeable level. Your current standard is the ceiling of your potential.

Burn the Boats Action Plan

This is your personal declaration of war on your old self. Take a moment, get a pen, and make this a physical act of commitment.

A Warning: The Fire Will Test You The moment you commit to burning a boat, your mind will rebel. It will scream at you with fear, doubt, and a desperate desire for the old comfort. This is normal. This is the addiction to your old self fighting back. Do not mistake this internal panic for a sign that you're making the wrong decision. It is the ultimate confirmation that you are finally doing something that matters. Your job is to feel that fear and take the action anyway.

1. **Identify Your #1 Boat to Burn:** What is the one habit, excuse, or belief that is the primary escape route back to your old life? Be specific.

- *My #1 Boat to Burn is:* ______________________________
____

1. **Define the Action:** What is the single, irreversible action you will take to burn this boat? This must be a decisive act, not a half-hearted attempt.

- *The Action to Burn It Is:* ______________________________
____

1. **Establish a Point of No Return:** What is the specific date or time by which this action will be completed? Write it down.

- *I Will Burn This Boat by:* ______________________________

---

1. **Declare Your Commitment:** Say this to yourself, out loud, and mean it. This is your oath.

- "I will no longer entertain the possibility of retreat. I will not go back to who I was. The bridges are burned, the ships are ablaze. My only option is to move forward and dominate. I am my own last resort."

Your life will not transform until you make this decision. There is no going back. There is no plan B. There is only a clear path forward, and the old you is a burning ship on the horizon.

13

Chapter 13: Momentum Over Motivation

Let me tell you another truth that will set you free: you are waiting for something that doesn't exist. You are waiting for the motivation to show up. You want to feel energized, inspired, and excited before you take action. You want to feel good.

And that's why you are stuck.

You have a choice to make: will you chase a feeling, or will you build a force?

The Flaw in the Motivation Model

Motivation is a lie. It's a fickle, emotional impulse that will leave you the moment a task gets hard, you feel tired, or your plan hits a wall. Motivation is what you have when you're watching a great speech. Momentum is what you have when you're already in the arena, swinging.

Relying on motivation is a losing strategy because your feelings are the most unreliable compass you will ever use. You don't have control over whether you *feel* like doing something. The world's most successful people don't wake up every day feeling like a winner. They feel tired. They feel discouraged. They feel just as much doubt as you do. The difference is they don't wait for a feeling to take action.

The person who waits for motivation to act will be a person who waits forever.

Momentum: The Unstoppable Force

Momentum is a powerful, self-sustaining force built by consistent action, not by fleeting inspiration. Think of a rocket launching into space. It takes a massive amount of fuel and fire to escape the gravitational pull of the Earth. It's a violent, difficult, and loud process. But once it breaks free, it cruises effortlessly through the vacuum of space.

Your life is a rocket launch. All the small, disciplined acts we've talked about—the daily checklist, the weekly plan, the goals you've set—are the fire and fuel you need to escape the gravity of your old habits.

You don't need to feel motivated to write the first sentence. You just need to write the first sentence. You don't need to feel motivated to go to the gym. You just need to put on your shoes and walk out the door. The motivation, the energy, and the drive will come *after* you start, not before. Your emotions will follow your actions. Not the other way around. This is the simple, undeniable secret to high performance.

This is a law of human psychology. It's called a **habit loop**:

1. **Cue:** Something triggers the action (e.g., your alarm goes off).
2. **Routine:** The action you take (e.g., getting out of bed immediately).
3. **Reward:** The positive feeling you get from the action (e.g., a sense of accomplishment, more energy).

Most people wait for the reward before they start the routine. A winner builds the routine and trusts that the reward will follow.

How to Build Unstoppable Momentum

1. **Kill the Big Task with a Small Win.** Stop looking at the entire mountain you have to climb. Focus on the very first step. If you want to write a book, don't think about the entire manuscript; think about writing for ten minutes. If you want to launch a business, don't think about the entire business plan; think about writing a single email. Momentum begins with a small, undeniable win.
2. **Stack the Wins.** Use your checklists and trackers to prove to yourself that you are in control. Every check mark is a win. Every win builds confidence. Every confident action builds momentum. The more wins you stack, the harder it becomes to break the chain.
3. **Don't Break the Chain.** Consistency is the fuel of momentum. The most powerful act you can do is show up every single day, no matter how you feel. It is your non-negotiable commitment to yourself. Your emotions will betray you. Your actions will not.

Stop waiting for a feeling. Start building a force. Your freedom is not found in the emotional high of motivation; it's found in the unstoppable forward motion of momentum.

14

Chapter 14: Small Win Streak Tracker & Don't Break the Chain Chart

You know the truth: motivation is a feeling, but momentum is a force. That force is built one day at a time, with one small win at a time. The problem is, it's easy to lose sight of your progress and slip back into old habits. Your mind can trick you into thinking your small efforts don't matter. This tracker is your antidote to that lie.

This tool turns your invisible momentum into a visible, undeniable streak. It's a simple, powerful visual representation of your commitment. The goal is simple: start a streak and don't break the chain. Every single day that you check a box, you're not just completing a task; you're building a habit, a foundation, and a winning mindset.

This is how you go from being someone who "tries" to being someone who **does**.

Use this chart as your personal scoreboard. Pin it somewhere you can't ignore it—on your wall, on your mirror, on the refrigerator. Let your commitment stare you in the face. The work begins now.

Small Win Streak Tracker

My #1 Small Win to Track: ________________________________

(e.g., "Workout," "Meditate," "Read 10 Pages," "No Social Media," "Work on Side Project")

Mon	Tue	Wed	Thu	Fri	Sat	Sun
☐	☐	☐	☐	☐	☐	☐

My #1 Small Win to Track: ________________________________

(e.g., "Workout," "Meditate," "Read 10 Pages," "No Social Media," "Work on Side Project")

Mon	Tue	Wed	Thu	Fri	Sat	Sun
☐	☐	☐	☐	☐	☐	☐

Don't Break the Chain

"My discipline is my freedom. My consistency is my power. I will not break the chain."

End of Week Reflection:

How did this week feel as the streak grew?

What was the biggest challenge to staying consistent?

- What is my new commitment for the week to come?

15

Chapter 15: Your 90-Day Deep Work Blueprint

You've used the tools. You've filled the trackers. You've mastered the art of discipline, embraced momentum over motivation, and you've burned the boats on your old self. You've audited your circle and started to take radical ownership of your mind and your money. You have been through the training. All of those lessons—every checkmark, every reflection, every act of courage—were not the end goal. They were preparation. This moment is the true test of your discipline and your radical ownership.

Most people want a finished blueprint handed to them. They want to be told exactly what to do, when to do it, and how to do it. They want a pre-made meal plan for success. But that is the mindset of a follower, and you are here to become a leader. The old you, the one who was stuck and playing small, is screaming right now. It wants a pre-packaged solution. It wants comfort. It wants to consume, not to create.

But you are not here to consume. You are here to build.

Your next-level self isn't a pre-packaged product. It's a

masterpiece you must design and build yourself. The ultimate act of discipline isn't following a plan; it's creating one. It's taking raw vision and turning it into a strategic, actionable blueprint. The act of creating your own plan forces you to think. It forces you to confront the obstacles you know you'll face. It forces you to take full, undeniable ownership of your mission. This is the difference between an employee and an entrepreneur. The former follows a plan. The latter creates one.

This is your mission: Stop reading. Take a blank page, a fresh notebook, or a new document. You are going to create your own 90-day Deep Work Planner from scratch. This isn't just an activity; it's your first major act of leadership on this new journey. It's the moment you stop being a passenger in your own life and start being the architect of your destiny.

The 90-Day Deep Work Blueprint Activity

Instructions: Get a blank page. Acknowledge that the canvas is yours. The lines you draw, the goals you set, and the plans you make are the ultimate proof of your commitment.

1. **Define Your 90-Day Mission:** At the very top of your page, write down **one** major project or mission you will dedicate yourself to for the next 90 days. Be specific. This is your target.
2. **Break It Down:** Divide your page into three distinct sections: **Days 1-30**, **Days 31-60**, and **Days 61-90**. Label each section. This is your strategic sprint.
3. **Set Your Milestones:** For each 30-day phase, define a major milestone you must hit to move the project forward. This is the goal for that phase.

4. **Create Your Tracking System:** For each day, create a clear, simple way to track your deep work sessions. This could be a checkmark, a box to write in your time, or a brief note on your progress.
5. **Build in a Feedback Loop:** At the end of each 30-day section, add a place for a reflection. Ask yourself, "What worked? What didn't? What is my new focus for the next 30 days?"

This is not a test to see if you can follow instructions. It is a test to see if you are a creator. It's a test of your discipline. It's a test of your ownership. The work begins now.

16

Chapter 16: 30-Day Become Undeniable Challenge Tracker

This is the final test. This is where you prove everything you've learned. For the next 30 days, you will build a life so full of purpose, discipline, and results that no one can question your potential or your success—not even yourself.

You've mastered the discipline of the daily grind. You've embraced momentum over motivation. You have a plan, a mission, and a deeper understanding of your purpose. Now, it's time to put all of those pieces together into a final, all-out sprint. Thirty days is not an arbitrary number. It is long enough to build a habit and cement a new identity, and it is short enough to maintain an unwavering, intense focus. This isn't just a challenge; it's a declaration.

Becoming "undeniable" is about building a body of work and a mindset that speaks for itself. It's about being so consistent and so focused that your results become your resume. You won't have to convince anyone of your work ethic, your commitment, or your power—your actions will do all the talking. This challenge is your opportunity to prove, once and for all, who you are and what you are capable of building.

This tracker is your scoreboard. Every day you complete the challenge, you are not just checking a box—you are building an unbreakable identity. You're not just doing the work; you are becoming the work. It's time to stop surviving and start dominating.

The final sprint begins now.

30-Day Become Undeniable Challenge Tracker

30-Day Become Undeniable Challenge Tracker

Instructions: Track your consistency, mindset, effort, and discipline daily. Check off each item you complete and rate your focus at the end of each day.

Day	Wake Up Early	No Excuses	Deep Work Done	Workou t	Rate Your Focus (1-10)
1	☐	☐	☐	☐	
2	☐	☐	☐	☐	
3	☐	☐	☐	☐	
4	☐	☐	☐	☐	
5	☐	☐	☐	☐	
6	☐	☐	☐	☐	
7	☐	☐	☐	☐	
8	☐	☐	☐	☐	
9	☐	☐	☐	☐	
10	☐	☐	☐	☐	
11	☐	☐	☐	☐	
12	☐	☐	☐	☐	

13	☐	☐	☐	☐
14	☐	☐	☐	☐
15	☐	☐	☐	☐
16	☐	☐	☐	☐
17	☐	☐	☐	☐
18	☐	☐	☐	☐
19	☐	☐	☐	☐
20	☐	☐	☐	☐
21	☐	☐	☐	☐
22	☐	☐	☐	☐
23	☐	☐	☐	☐
24	☐	☐	☐	☐
25	☐	☐	☐	☐
26	☐	☐	☐	☐
27	☐	☐	☐	☐
28	☐	☐	☐	☐
29	☐	☐	☐	☐
30	☐	☐	☐	☐

17

Final Chapter: Radical Ownership

No more blame. No more waiting. No more excuses.

To fully grasp the power of Radical Ownership, you must first look its enemy in the eye: The Victim Mindset.

The victim lives a life of reaction. When they fail, it's the economy's fault, their boss's fault, or their upbringing's fault. Their language is filled with 'if only' and 'they should have.' They wait for permission, they wait for perfect conditions, and they wait for someone else to save them. The victim outsources responsibility for their life and, in doing so, outsources their power.

Radical Ownership is the declaration that you will no longer be a victim of your own life. You are the cause, not the effect.

You have now reached the end of this book, but you are only at the beginning of your journey. The chapters, the checklists, the trackers, the moments of discomfort—they were all designed for this singular moment. The moment you stop being a passenger in your own life and take the wheel. The moment you step fully into Radical Ownership.

Radical ownership isn't a partial commitment. It isn't taking responsibility for your wins but blaming others for your losses. It is the uncompromising, unapologetic truth that your life—every outcome, every opportunity, and every obstacle—is a direct result of your decisions. Your energy is your decision. Your future is your decision. Your fire is your decision.

I remember a time, even after starting this journey, when a major client project fell through. The old me would have had a list of excuses ready: the market shifted, the client was indecisive, my team didn't execute. And all of it would have been partially true. But at that moment, I made a different choice. I sat down with my journal and wrote, 'This is my fault.' I owned it. I owned the fact that I hadn't communicated the value clearly enough. I owned that I hadn't anticipated the market shift. I thought that I hadn't trained my team well enough. That act of ownership was painful, but it was also incredibly powerful. It stopped the bleeding of blame and immediately shifted my focus from 'Whose fault is this?' to 'What am I going to do about it?' It gave me back the wheel. That is the power you are claiming today.

You didn't get here overnight. The habits that kept you stuck were built over time. But you can turn the tide today. The decision to take radical ownership is the single most powerful act of leadership you can make. It is the final brick in the foundation we have been building.

Owning everything means:

- You stop outsourcing your power. You no longer look for a miracle, a lucky break, or a perfect plan. You understand that your power lies in your own hands.
- You take charge of your time. You stop giving away your mornings, your weekends, and your potential to things that

don't matter. Your time is a resource you will no longer tolerate wasting.

- You lead your mind, your money, and your movement. You are the captain of your ship. You command your thoughts, you direct your resources, and you are the engine of your own momentum.

This book is not just something to read. It's a manual for action. Every chapter you've read, every page you've filled, every tracker you've completed—has been about reclaiming that fire. Your next-level self isn't a fantasy. It's a decision.

Now burn the excuses. Build the habits. Reclaim your fire.

You are not waiting on a miracle. The miracle is you.

Own it.

18

Conclusion

THE OWNERS OATH

This is your new creed. Read it. Say it aloud. Let it be the operating system for the rest of your life.
My mind is my responsibility. My actions are my responsibility. My results are my responsibility. I am not a victim of my circumstances. I am the architect of my destiny. I own my life.

Afterword

If you've made it this far, it's because something inside of you is done settling. Done waiting. Done wishing. Done playing small.

Let this book be a launchpad, not a lullaby. You don't need a perfect plan. You need persistent fire.

Every chapter you've read, every page you've filled, every tracker you've completed—has been about reclaiming that fire. Your next-level self isn't a fantasy. It's a decision.

You're no longer allowed to stay stuck, scared, or silent.

From this day forward:

- Own your mornings.
- Move with purpose.
- Speak like a leader.
- Build like your legacy depends on it—because it does.

Don't just live. Lead.

Don't just hope. Hunt.

Don't just try. Transform.

The world doesn't need more noise.

It needs more you.

Stay bold. Stay excited.

Stay dangerous.

We're not here to survive. We're here to dominate.

Let's go.

— Dr. Gerald W. Parker

About the Author

Dr. Gerald W. Parker is a transformational speaker, mentor, and visionary leader committed to helping people unleash their potential, reclaim their fire, and live lives that are both profitable and purposeful. With decades of experience in coaching, leadership development, and personal mastery, Dr. Parker brings a no-excuses, high-impact message to audiences worldwide. He is also a success coach and a passionate advocate for personal ownership.

A firm believer in radical ownership and unapologetic excitement, he teaches that you don't have to wait for the perfect moment—you create it. His coaching has empowered thousands to break through limiting beliefs, ignite discipline, and step fully into the lives they were meant to live. Dr. Parker's mission is simple: Help you stop surviving and start building a life that pays you back.

This book is more than pages—it's a personal challenge, a movement, and a manifesto.

www.ingramcontent.com/pod-product-compliance
Lightning Source LLC
LaVergne TN
LVHW090333210926
848480LV00004B/1392